ACTIV

CARTOONING

Illustrated by Tim Benton
Written by Kate Brookes

Hodder
Children's
Books

a division of Hodder Headline plc

With lots of thanks to Anne Clark (who got the ball rolling), cartoonist David Farris (for keeping it in play), Joy Mutter (for designing the team's away-match strip) and Bob Murray (for putting the ball into the back of the net).

Series design by Fiona Webb
Book design by Joy Mutter
Cover illustration by David Farris

Printed by Clays Ltd, St Ives plc

Hodder Children's Books
a division of Hodder Headline plc
338 Euston Road
London NW1 3BH

Meet the team

When Kate Brookes – great writer, lousy doodler – met Tim Benton – cartoonist par excellence – they quickly realised they were the perfect match. Each had something the other wanted. Kate could write, Tim could draw – and both wanted to produce a book that would unlock the secrets of cartooning so that anyone could do it.

Once some urgent chores like putting out the cat, sorting the sock drawer, writing *Life, Love and High Marks* and illustrating Activators *Internet* were done, they started working on *Cartooning*. And what fun it turned out to be.

While Kate's computer hummed into life, Tim sharpened his pencils and went out to buy a new eraser. Then it all happened. A book came to life. Before Kate's eyes, Tim turned boring squares into roaring lions, triangles became crying footballers and circles finished up as dancing teapots. And all the while, Kate took pages of notes about how it was done.

Kate can now draw cartoons, Tim is a happy cartoonist and both Kate and Tim hope you have as much fun reading this book as they did putting it together.

Introduction

So you want to be able to draw cartoons? Good. The world needs more cartoons. Cartoons make us laugh. They are fun to look at and fun to draw. And best of all, you can draw them. A few pages into this book and you will be drawing cartoons that will amaze your family and friends.

To be a cartoonist all you need is imagination, powers of observation, a sense of humour, a pencil, some paper and an eraser (even the best cartoonists make mistakes) – and this book.

We aim to give you tips, explain the shortcuts and provide plenty of ideas, but what you draw is up to you. There are no rules. If you want a drawing of the headteacher to have three heads, then that's fine. Mind you, the headteacher won't be too impressed!

So say goodbye to the matchstick people you used to draw because from now on you're going to be an ace cartoonist!

Contents

Getting started

Look at the drawings on these pages. Notice anything about them? A clue is the dotted lines. That's right, all the characters fit into a shape – a circle, an oval, a triangle, a rectangle or a square. This family of shapes is behind all the best cartoon characters. If you can draw them – and let's face it, most people can – it's only a hop, a skip and a jump to drawing cartoons.

So starting now, before you draw anything, first lightly draw the shapes that your subject consists of – an oval for a frog, a triangle for a cat and so on. Once you have these shapes on paper, it will be easier to bring your characters to life.

Tim has drawn in the main shapes that form the basis of the pictures here. But there are lots more smaller shapes. In fact, just about everything that goes into a cartoon picture can be based on one of our five shapes. Using tracing paper, draw these funny faces using only squares, ovals circles, triangles and rectangles.

Cartoon gallery

Throughout this book there are gallery pages that are bursting with great cartoon ideas. In this gallery, Tim has drawn the basic shapes that hide under some finished cartoons.

The king of the beasts is just a circle and a triangle

Ducks and superheroes have a lot in common – triangles!

Find the basic shapes and you can drawn anything

CAPTAIN TRIANGLE

What you need

Most of the things you'll need to be a cartoonist you will have already. What you don't have, or can't find in the bottom of your school bag, you can buy from stationery or art shops. There's nothing that a little pocket money won't pay for.

Pencils

You probably thought a pencil is a pencil is a pencil, but you'd be wrong. Pencils are given ratings that indicate how strong or faint their lines are. Use a 2H pencil for drawing very light lines that you want to rub out, for example the lines for the basic shapes. A 2B or 3B pencil makes a good strong line for creating finished cartoons or for adding shading.

Pens

Forget about ballpoint pens – they drop blobs of ink in the most embarrassing places and they smudge. Much better are felt-tipped or plastic-tipped pens. You can buy them in different thicknesses from fine to thick. The only trick to establishing a long-term relationship with a felt-tipped pen is remembering to replace the cap!

Paper

As long as there's room for you to doodle, any piece of paper will do – cartoonists have been known to draw on the fish and chip paper! The most important thing is not what you draw on but having lots of it. To start with, try inexpensive, recycled paper but if the cartooning bug really bites, add a pad of cartridge paper to your birthday wish-list.

Layout/tracing paper

Inexpensive layout paper is good to draw on and because you can see through it, you can use it for tracing. You can buy layout pads in large stationery shops and all art shops. If it's just tracing you want to do, raid the kitchen for a roll of cooking parchment paper or baking paper. (To find out how to transfer tracings to paper, see page 83.)

Eraser

The best sort is a soft, vinyl eraser. Putty rubbers are not very effective at rubbing out 2H pencil lines, and ink rubbers are so hard they'll bore holes in your drawings.

Pencil sharpener

Not much point to drawing if your pencil's blunt.

Trade secret

Cartoonists are always making mistakes and so over the years they have come up with some sneaky ways of hiding them. One of the best is to simply paint over with white correction fluid – the stuff that comes in little plastic bottles and hardens to concrete if you leave the lid off. Apply the correction fluid smoothly and sparingly and remember to wait for it to dry completely before drawing on it. If this doesn't do the job, cut out a piece of paper and glue it over the mistake. When you photocopy the finished illustration, any cover-ups will be undetectable.

Warming up

Even though geometric shapes are used as the scaffolding on which all cartoons are built, you don't have to use rulers or compasses to draw them. Cartooning is a freehand art of flowing lines drawn with great oooomph! To get into the swing of things, practise these drawings.

Cloud

STEP 1

Before even putting your 2H pencil to paper, practise drawing the oval shape in the air. Once you've got the hang of the movement, quickly and lightly draw the oval on the paper.

STEP 2

Now that you've got the basic shape, lightly draw in the detail of the fluffy cloud using lots of small arcs.

STEP 3

Go over the lines you want to keep with a felt-tipped pen. When dry, rub out any pencil lines.

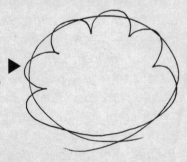

STEP 4

Add the sun peeping out from behind the cloud. You've just done your first cartoon! OK, so the cloud didn't make you laugh, but you've got to start somewhere.

Tree

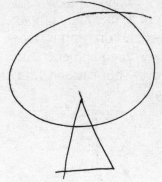

STEP 1
Draw the basic circle and triangle that make up a tree. As before, practise the movements in the air before you draw them on paper.

STEP 2
Draw a rough outline of the foliage – that's the green stuff at the top of the trunk.

STEP 3
Give the foliage more detail and draw branches at the top of the trunk. When you think you've got it right, go over with a felt-tipped pen and rub out the pencil lines.

STEP 4
Put your tree in a setting by drawing tufts of spiky grass around the base. Told you this cartooning business was easy, and, yes, it will start to get funny very soon.

Cool Charlie

Charlie's so cool because he's so easy to draw. You can draw his basic shapes with the help of a ruler and compass, or you can do them freehand. A freehand drawing is done without rulers or other pieces of drawing equipment. Do steps 1 to 5 in pencil and then go over your cartoon with a felt-tipped pen.

STEP 1 ▲

Draw a circle and a rectangle. The circle should fit into the rectangle about twice.

STEP 2 ▲

Add arms and legs. Divide the circle into quarters. This will help you position facial features.

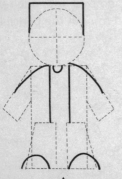

STEP 3 ▲

Now that Charlie's shape is outlined, fill in details like hair, shoulders, neckline and shoes.

STEP 4 ▲

Draw lines for the nose, mouth, ears and clothing. Have you noticed that Charlie is symmetrical

8

STEP 5 ▲

Draw lines to add more detail to the face and clothing.

STEP 6 ▲

Finish Charlie by going over him with a felt-tipped pen. Rub out any pencil lines.

Practise, practise, practise

Great cartoonists and artists practise their craft, that's why they're so good at it. To invent a character like Cool Charlie, Tim spent hours getting him just right. Ten generations of Charlies ended up in the bin, and with each new Charlie, his expression, posture and clothing were changed. To create your first cartoon character, use Charlie's basic shape but give him a different look. Very soon you'll be drawing your own version of Charlie freehand using rough outlines of the basic shapes. Go to it!

Cartoon gallery

The good thing about squares, triangles and circles is that you can squash them and stretch them to create lots of different shapes. Can you spot the squashed squares, trampled triangles and crushed circles in these cartoons?

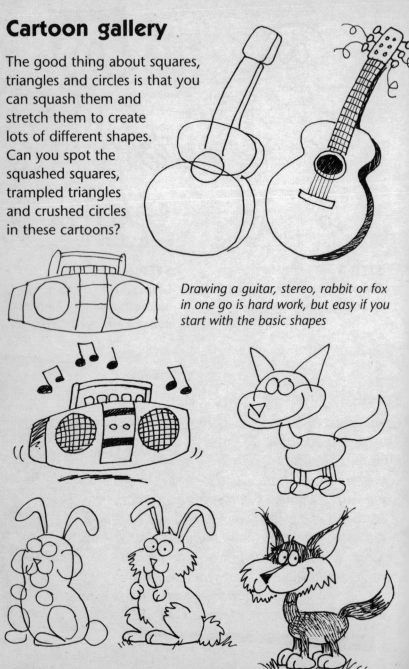

Drawing a guitar, stereo, rabbit or fox in one go is hard work, but easy if you start with the basic shapes

Giving your cartoons depth is easy when you start with the basic shapes

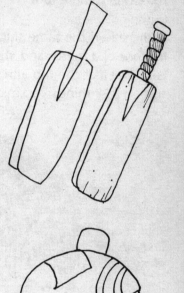

Know why they're known as sausage dogs?

The basic shape of a trainer is an oval cut in half

2 Drawing faces

One of the brilliant things about cartoons is that they don't have to be realistic. Cartoon faces can be as wild and as wacky as you like. But it still helps if you learn the basics of drawing a 'real' face first. It makes breaking the rules much more fun!

Your head is the same shape as an egg. Hold an egg, stand in front of a mirror and check it out. An egg, like your head, is rounded at the top and pointy at the bottom. Here are some other things you might not know about yourself:

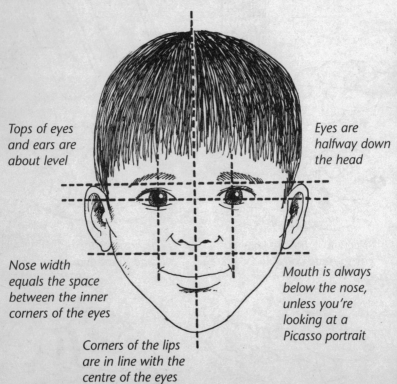

Tops of eyes and ears are about level

Eyes are halfway down the head

Nose width equals the space between the inner corners of the eyes

Mouth is always below the nose, unless you're looking at a Picasso portrait

Corners of the lips are in line with the centre of the eyes

12

What makes each face different?

Cartoonists create totally unique faces because they can distort and exaggerate the shape and details. This isn't done to create just funny-looking faces but to establish character and to show, without words, whether the face is laughing, crying, scared or angry. Look at the faces below and see if you can pick the telling differences between them. All have two eyes, two ears, a nose and a mouth but that's all they have in common!

Mr Miserable – who said heads had to be round?

Miss Prim – hair can say a lot

Mr Mischief – you can do a lot with a few teeth

Ms Menace – have you ever seen meaner eyes?

Mr Worry – worry lines aplenty!

Capturing facial expressions

Look in the mirror and watch how the shape and position of your eyes, mouth and eyebrows alter when you change your expression. Try going from a cheery "My team won the match" smile to a "Sprouts again for dinner" look of disgust. Without your even saying a word, your face shows your mood. Being able to draw lots of different expressions will make your cartoons come to life and help you tell a story. Look at the expressions on the faces in this cartoon – each is different and tells us something about the character.

Trade secret

*Cartoonists are the snoops of the
art world – they are rarely seen
without a sketchbook and pencil
ready to record people's expressions,
posture, dress and movements. Get
into the habit of carrying a small sketchbook
and pencil with you whenever you go out.*

Laughing Len

STEP 1

Draw the outline of the head in pencil. Note how the oval tilts a little to one side.

▶

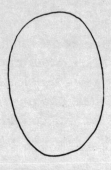

◀ **STEP 2**

Draw circles for the cheeks, nose and ears. The mouth is an oval that has sagged at the top.

STEP 3

The eyes are just lines radiating from above the nose. Draw eyebrows and smile lines high on the forehead.

▶

◀ **STEP 4**

Add detail to the ears by drawing a number 5 (one is drawn backwards) inside the ear circles.

◀ **STEP 5**
Line the mouth with teeth.
Make the front teeth larger
than the back teeth.

STEP 6 ▶
Go over with felt-tipped pen and
colour in the hair and the inside
of the mouth.

◀ **STEP 7**
Add movement lines and
tears (but not too many)
and Laughing Len will look
like he has just heard the
best joke ever. Rub out any
pencil lines.

Telling eyebrows

*Eyebrows are one of the cartoonist's
best friends since they can tell us
a lot about how a person is feeling.
Not bad for just a line or two!
They can be happy, sad, worried,
angry or just plain. Whatever the
mood, keep them as simple as
possible. Here are some ideas:*

Normal eyebrows

Happy eyebrows

Angry eyebrows

17

Boo-hoo Barney

STEP 1 ▲

Draw the outline of a head. Did you notice it's a slightly different shape from the laughing head?

STEP 2 ▲

Use circles, a semi-circle and a triangle for the ears, mouth and nose.

STEP 3 ▲

Draw short, straight lines for the eyes and curved lines for the eyebrows. See how close the eyes are to the nose.

STEP 4 ▲

Rub out the line inside the semicircle to create the down-turned mouth. Add detail to the ears.

STEP 5 ▲

Draw in a few teeth on the upper jaw. Add some hair.

STEP 6 ▲
Go over your cartoon
with felt-tipped pen
and colour in the hair
and mouth. When dry,
rub out any pencil lines.

STEP 7 ▲
Flood of tears and a mournful
"Boo, hoo!" finish this sad
cartoon character.

How to draw eyes

*Scared, bored, tired, sad, angry –
whatever your cartoon character
is up to, a big part of the success
in drawing it depends on getting
the eyes right. Practise the
different eye-deas shown here*

*along with
other styles
you see in
the book.
Label and
keep for
reference.*

Scared, alert eyes

Bored eyes

Tired eyes

Frightened Fred

STEP 1
Draw the outline of a
head in pencil.

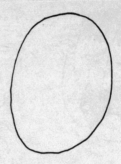

◀ **STEP 2**
Use circles, ovals and
lines for the features
on the face.

STEP 3
Draw a line to link the
nose with one eye, and
a wiggly line inside the
oval mouth.

◀ **STEP 4**
Draw eyebrows that curve
up towards the centre of
the forehead, and add
details to the ears.

◀ STEP 5

Two tiny dots are all that's needed for the pupils. Draw worry lines beside both eyes.

STEP 6 ▶

Draw quick lines to create the uprush of hair. Colour in the mouth.

◀ STEP 7

Draw "shock, horror" lines around the face. Go over with felt-tipped pen. When dry, rub out pencil lines.

When you smile ...

We all know that happy mouths turn up at the corners and sad mouths turn down. But there is a lot more you can do with the mouth to convey what your character is feeling. Draw all the different mouths you can find and label them.

Braced for a smile

The big sulk

Ooo! The surprised mouth

21

Angry Alice

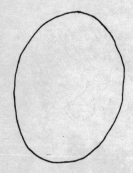

STEP 1 ▲

Draw the outline of a head in pencil.

STEP 2 ▲

An angry face is quite complicated even when it is reduced to simple shapes.

STEP 3 ▲

The eyebrows are sharply angled lines that cut across the eyes. The vertical line between the eyes is an angry forehead!

STEP 4 ▲

Draw the number 5 – one is drawn backward – inside each ear to add detail.

◀ STEP 5

The pupils are dots positioned right under each eyebrow. Draw in the hair.

STEP 6 ▶

Keep your distance – this girl is about to blow! Anger lines zap beside her eyes, steam rises from her head, and her teeth (drawn like window panes) are grinding.

Noses are easy

Cartoon noses are easy to draw. All you have to decide is whether the nose – small or large – will be bulbous and droopy, cute and round, or pointy and pert. Just make sure you match the nose to the sort of character you're drawing. A witch with a cute button nose just doesn't seem right, does it?

Noses from the front and side

Cartoons are useful things

OK, so you can't fly to the moon with a cartoon or use one to mend a puncture on your bike, but you can use cartoons to cheer up friends and family and to decorate your room. And if you really want to impress, how about designing and illustrating your own address card? To write messages on your cards or posters, read up about lettering in Chapter 7.

Cards

Use your cartoons (or trace some of Tim's) to design your own special range of birthday cards, get well cards, party invites, and "Oops, I'm sorry" cards. All you need is some blank clean card (white or coloured), drawing tools and a good idea. Cut and fold your cards so that they will fit inside ready-made envelopes. Your friends will love them – and you have saved the cost of buying a card!

3-D Keep Out Poster

To make a cartoon illustration look as though it is three-dimensional, you need three identical copies (photocopies or tracings are fine) of the cartoon, three small squares of thick card, glue, scissors and a piece of card onto which your cartoons can be mounted. Neatly cut out the cartoons and glue a piece of thick card onto the back of each one. Glue one cartoon onto the mounting card, and then glue the remaining cartoons on top so that part of the previous cartoon is visible. Do the same for the lettering on the poster. Draw a simple background scene directly on the card.

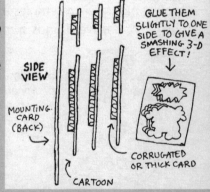

SIDE VIEW

MOUNTING CARD (BACK)

CARTOON

GLUE THEM SLIGHTLY TO ONE SIDE TO GIVE A SMASHING 3-D EFFECT!

CORRUGATED OR THICK CARD

Address card

Address cards are only small (6cm by 9cm) but there's a lot of information that has to be squeezed on. You need to include your name, address and phone number, and maybe even an e-mail address. Decorate your address card with a cartoon of yourself. When you've designed and illustrated your card, make photocopies and trim them to size. Then all you have to do is give them out to everyone you know.

GARY THE GREAT

HIYA!

13 STINKY STREET
OLD SOCKFORD
TEL: 01123 546
EMAIL: GARY@
SMELLYTWERP.COM.

What hair-do for you?

You can really let yourself go when giving your cartoon characters a head of hair. There are no rules, just lots of different styles to try. You could make the hair suit your character or you could make it totally contrast. For example, you could draw a friendly teacher with a short bob, a serious businessman sporting a punk mohawk, or a beefy sailor with pigtails and bows.

Always draw the face and all the important features before you draw the outline of the hair. To give the hair texture and movement, draw it using quick, light pencil strokes. Even the neatest hair rarely resembles a tin helmet, so make the ends uneven and leave strands sprouting from the top of the head.

It is always worth experimenting with different styles for different faces

Hair can be straight, curly or tightly-coiled

Hair is great for making jokes. The beefy chap above doesn't look pleased with his pigtails!

Hair flair gallery

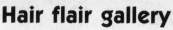

The hairstyle can tell a lot about the character

Teacher and teacher's pet

*Big hair ...
... no hair*

Mad hair day!

Simply shocking!

An easy hairstyle to draw on a face in profile

Oodles of curls

Slicked-down hair catches the light

27

Got a head, get a hat

Hats not only give a cartoon person a
character but can also show what
job they do, where they're from
and even when they lived. A hat worn
at a jaunty angle and almost covering
the eyes is a give-away for a spy or
villain, and a tiny hat perched on a
large, round face instantly turns its
owner into a comic character.

*Which
way's the
Wild West?*

Le beret

*Back-to-front
baseball cap*

Flat-cap Fred

*Viking
worrier*

*Tiny hat for a
comic and a large
one for a chef*

Tell-tale details

There's an endless number of
ways that you can reveal the
character of your cartoon
people. Some of these are
really obvious – like warts
for a witch or an eyepatch
for a pirate. Other things
you can use include beards,
moustaches and spectacles.
What do the details tell you
about these characters?

*Who else but
a pirate?*

*What makes
you think he's
a swimmer?*

*Specs turn
boy into
brain-box*

*Do you think
he's ill?*

*An artist's
moustache*

*Steer clear
of warty nose*

*Lots of rings
for this boy*

Faces from different views

When you draw a face front on, the cartoon character is "talking" just to you, the viewer. To get your characters to talk or react to each other, you have to draw their faces from different angles. Being able to draw faces from different angles also lets you show different postures and emotions. A shy person, for example, will look down and almost bury their head into their chest, while a snooty person holds their head high and looks down their nose at you.

Profile view

STEP 1 ▶
Draw the outline and divide it into quarters. These lines help you position the ear, eye, cheek, nose and mouth.

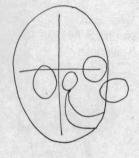
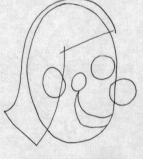

STEP 2 ▲
Draw in a rough outline of the hair.

STEP 3 ▶
Start drawing in detail for the hair. Draw in an eyebrow.

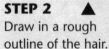

STEP 4 ▶
Finish the ear and draw a dot for the pupil. Add quick strokes to the hair to give texture. Go over with felt-tipped pen and rub out pencil lines.

Three-quarter view

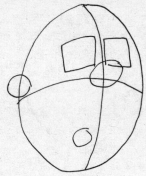

STEP 1 ▲

Draw the outline and curved guidelines as shown. Draw the basic shapes for the eyes (square because the character is wearing glasses), nose, mouth and one ear.

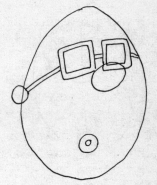

STEP 2 ▲

Add detail to the glasses and mouth. This mouth shape is round and shows surprise.

STEP 3 ▲

Draw the chubby chin, raised eyebrows and ear detail.

STEP 4 ▲

Make small dots for the eyes. Dark, curly hair sits close to the head. Shade in some areas to give the face colour and shape. Go over with felt-tipped pen and rub out pencil lines.

Drawing faces

Looking up

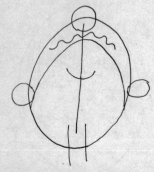

STEP 1 ▲

Draw the outline and
guidelines as shown in pencil.
Then draw the neck, chin, ears,
wiggly moustache and nose.

STEP 2 ▲

Draw nostrils and a curved line
under the moustache for the
mouth. Add detail to the ears.
Go over with felt-tipped pen
and rub out pencil lines.

Looking down

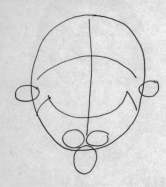

STEP 1 ▲

Draw the outline and guidelines
as shown in pencil. Draw rough
shapes for the ears and face area.
Inside the face area, draw eyes
and nose.

STEP 2 ▲

Draw a mop of hair radiating
from the centre of the head.
Add details to the face,
making sure the eyes are
looking down.

32

Neck and shoulders

Even cartoon characters need
something for their head to sit
on – unless, of course, they're Anne
Boleyn or the Headless Horseman!

Neck and shoulders determine the
build and posture of your character.
In cartoonland, bodybuilders have
necks like tree trunks and shoulders
like boulders but wimps with
lolly-stick necks can barely hold
their head up.

*Large Adam's apple
always looks funny*

*Chin and neck
have become one*

*This neck has
disappeared*

*You can even draw
a pretty neck!*

*To exaggerate the
head, rest it on a
skinny neck and
narrow shoulders*

33

How to use light and shade

To give your cartoons a really professional look, give them the light and shade treatment. Make areas in shadow dark using lots of fine lines – this is called cross-hatching – and other areas light. In this cartoon, cross-hatching is used to make the character's dark hair and to show which areas of the face are in shadow.

STEP 1 ▶

Draw the head and face using simple shapes and lines. With the light coming from the right, the left-hand side of the face will be in shadow. Lightly cross-hatch these areas.

STEP 2 ▶

Add cross-hatching in the opposite direction to make some areas darker. The light will highlight the texture of the hair, so draw in some curls.

STEP 3 ▶

Draw fine lines, in just one direction, across the hair. Make the lines closer when you get to the areas that are in shadow.

STEP 4 ▶

Cross-hatch the hair in the other direction. Don't forget that in areas of shadow, the lines must be closer together. Add light shadows to the left side of the eyes and nose.

Funny faces gallery

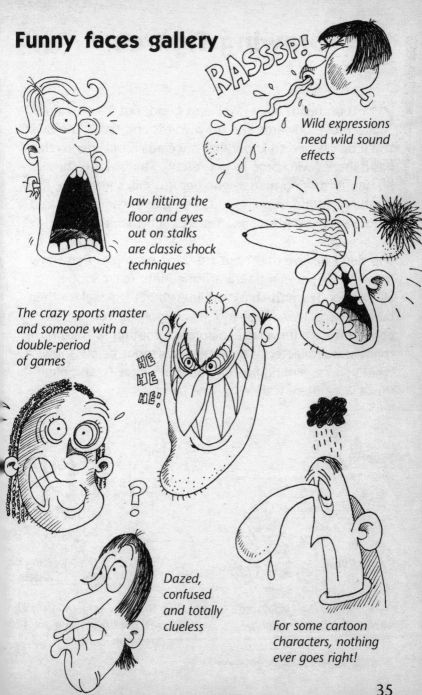

RASSSP!

Wild expressions need wild sound effects

Jaw hitting the floor and eyes out on stalks are classic shock techniques

The crazy sports master and someone with a double-period of games

HE HE HE!

Dazed, confused and totally clueless

For some cartoon characters, nothing ever goes right!

35

3 Drawing figures

Cartoon heads are all well and good, but it's now time to move onwards and downwards and tackle the BODY! You'll be pleased to know that once again our friends the basic shapes will come to our rescue. That's right, the human form – no matter whether it is tall, short, thin, fat, standing, sitting, running or falling over – can be reduced to just a few simple circles, squares and triangles.

You don't believe me? Here are some examples that show how the shapes can be transformed into real cartoon characters. Trace the basic outlines to get the feel for them before trying them freehand. It is important you are confident with the shapes before attempting to transform them into characters. The finished cartoons below show what you are aiming for but you don't have to complete those yet – there is time for that later!

From this ...

... to this ...

... by way of five circles and a triangle. That's my baby!

Two triangles, a rectangle and an oval are the starting point for our hippy friend

A basic figure, step-by-step

STEP 1 ▶
Use a pencil to
draw a simple
body and head.

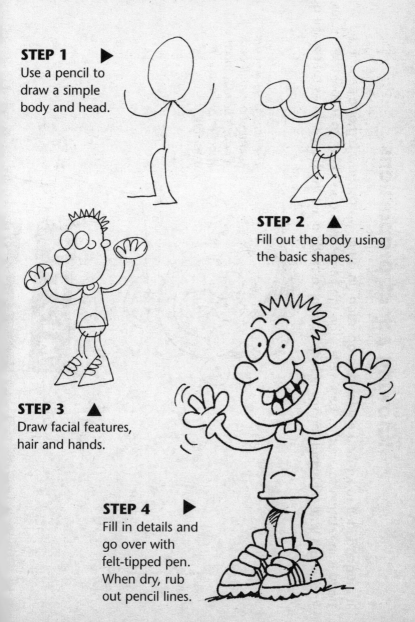

STEP 2 ▲
Fill out the body using
the basic shapes.

STEP 3 ▲
Draw facial features,
hair and hands.

STEP 4 ▶
Fill in details and
go over with
felt-tipped pen.
When dry, rub
out pencil lines.

Knowing about proportions

It's a good idea to know the rules of proportion (in other words, how big one part of the body is in relation to another part). Even though cartoonists don't have to follow these rules, knowing a little bit about them will help you to correctly draw the basic shapes that make up your cartoon.

The head is 1/6th of the height of an adult body. A baby's head is much larger in proportion to its height

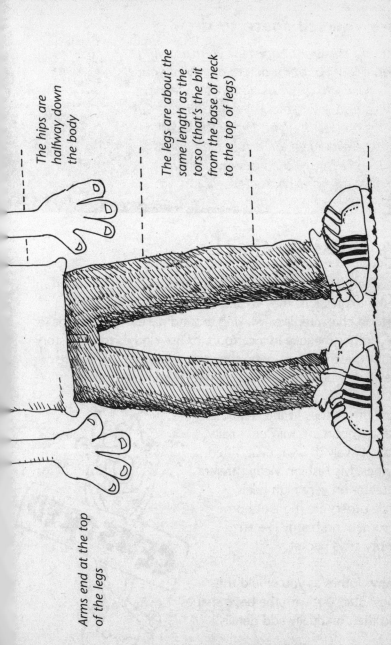

The hips are halfway down the body

The legs are about the same length as the torso (that's the bit from the base of neck to the top of legs)

Arms end at the top of the legs

Now that you know all about correct proportions, you can go about getting them totally wrong!

Give yourself space to draw

Use big sheets of paper for your drawings and allow your characters plenty of space. It's easier to draw using large, sweeping lines and it will mean you won't run out of room for the feet. Draw the head first, follow the $^1/6$th rule (see pages 38-39) and you'll know exactly how tall your character will be.

It's dress-up time!

How you dress your cartoon characters is almost as important as the expressions they wear. Besides, no self-respecting cartoon character likes walking around naked! You can make the clothes the joke in a cartoon, or use clothes to tell a story about the character – who they are, what they do, where they live, when they lived, or what their interests are.

How the clothes fit the character is also important. Mr Punctuality is most likely to wear neat, fitted clothes, Ms Fashion Victim prefers to teeter on very high heels, while others are more at home in something baggy like an empty crisp packet.

Draw clothes as you would the body. Start out with the basic shapes and then gradually add details.

40

Clothes, just like the body, can be reduced to basic shapes to make drawing them easy

Make some items of clothing dark by using patterns of lines

You don't have to show every button and stitch. Draw just those things (the fewer the better) that make it clear what your character is wearing

Work out what accessories your character will need when you first create it. It's hard to add things like hats, goggles – or ice hammer and flag – at the end

41

Clothes gallery

Pick and choose clothes for your characters from among these racks of bargain basement items.

Use the ideas here to make the clothes fit the characters you draw. Often the simplest ideas are the most effective, like the easy collar and tie (below)

DO YOU LIKE IT DEAR?

43

How to draw hands

If you want your cartoon characters to do something, then give them a pair of hands, not a bunch of bananas. With hands they can point, push buttons, wave, catch a ball and pick their nose. When drawing cartoon hands, don't get bogged down with fiddly wrinkles, nails and rings, just keep the shapes simple so that it's easy to see the gesture or movement. Rounded, sausage-like fingers are the easiest to draw and can be used for most characters. Long, pointy and angular fingers are best for evil types like mad scientists, witches and vampires.

Don't forget that if you are drawing a hand that is coming toward you, you should exaggerate its size.

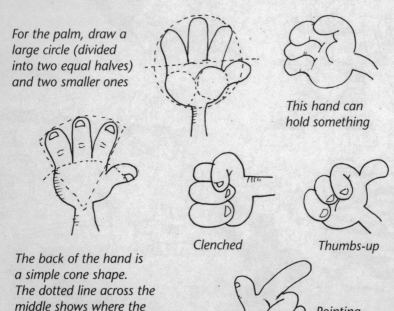

For the palm, draw a large circle (divided into two equal halves) and two smaller ones

This hand can hold something

The back of the hand is a simple cone shape. The dotted line across the middle shows where the fingers meet the hand

Clenched

Thumbs-up

Pointing

Practise drawing some simple hands, using the basic shapes to start. Then go on to draw hands that do something

Once you've got the hang of drawing hands, you can start to give them something to do like taking a crisp or picking a flower. To work out how to draw hands in different positions, use your non-cartooning hand as the model.

The trick to drawing hands that are attached to arms is making sure that the hands face the right way. Work this out by once again using yourself as the model.

Trade secret

Cartoonists and animation artists often draw only three fingers and a thumb on each hand. They do this to keep the drawing as simple and uncluttered as possible. Next time you watch an animated cartoon on television, pay close attention to the hands and how they are drawn.

45

How to draw feet

Feet can't say as much in a cartoon as hands and fingers, but they still do have great comic potential. You can give a tiny character enormous feet or a muscle man dainty feet. But whatever the size, remember that in cartoonland, feet only ever have four toes. You can draw the toes big, though, and also exaggerate the size of the heels.

The shape of a foot viewed from above is a triangle. And from below, circles and ovals.

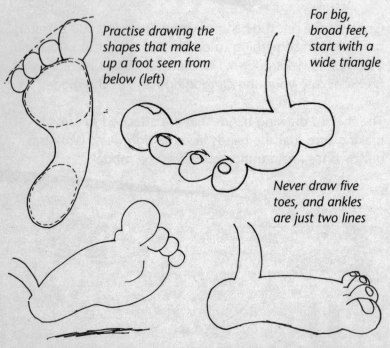

Practise drawing the shapes that make up a foot seen from below (left)

For big, broad feet, start with a wide triangle

Never draw five toes, and ankles are just two lines

The easiest way to show that a foot is moving is to draw a shadow under it

From the side, the basic shape of a foot is a rectangle

Shoe gallery

Shoes can tell a lot about your character and are a lot easier
to draw than clothes. The rules are, keep them simple and
don't overdo the detail, but exaggerate the features that
make them different – high heels, for example. Here are
some ideas – don't forget to start with the basic shapes!

*High heels or
trainers? Whiff
lines are a neat
trick; black with
a white patch
shows shiny
shoes*

47

Backgrounds for your cartoon characters

Just as actors on a stage need scenery, cartoon characters need a background. The background is an important part of a cartoon but it should never dominate your characters. A kitchen, for example, can be drawn by simply including a few pots and pans hanging from hooks on a non-existent wall, and a classroom by including a blackboard covered with white writing. The motto is – less is best. A city skyline can be changed to depict any city in the world simply by inserting a building that is associated with it. For example, the Eiffel Tower for Paris or the Statue of Liberty for New York.

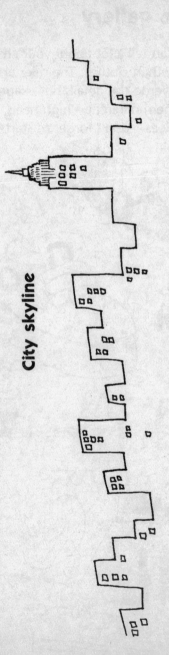

City skyline

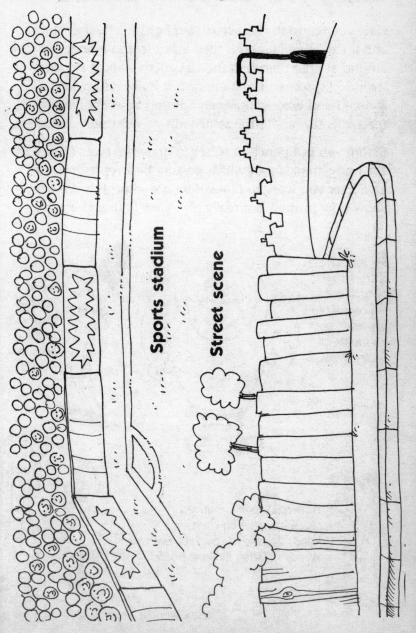

Sports stadium

Street scene

Giving your characters posture

How your cartoon characters stand or sit is their posture and it can say a lot about their attitude and mood. Just look around at your friends in the classroom – some slouch over their desks, some sit bolt upright. It is always obvious who is bored and who is totally enraptured by everything the teacher is saying. It's the same with your cartoon characters.

Before you put pencil to paper to draw the basic shapes of the body, think about which posture best represents the character you want to draw. Here are some Tim drew to show how posture can really give your figures character.

Big Ben – his posture says "Watch out, I'm coming to get you!" but his face is all smiles. Phew!

Proud Peter – chest out, shoulders back and chin high

Worried Wendy – rounded shoulders, chin on chest and hands deep in her pockets. Even Wendy's clothes look miserable!

Use a hunched-over posture to show ag

How to make a character fall over

Before you get your characters walking and running, you have to know about balance. If a figure is balanced, the head will be directly above the centre of the feet. You can draw pencil lines to help show this. The bendy dotted line through the gymnast suggests she is out of balance but (like all good gymnasts) she is perfectly balanced. Hold a ruler vertically against her head and feet to check.

Being unbalanced is not a bad thing. It's really handy if you want to show someone about to fall over. The boy below has his head and feet so far on either side of the straight balance line that you just know he's about to topple!

A head directly over the feet shows that despite her bendy body, this gymnast is perfectly in balance

Watch out, this guy is really unbalanced. His head and feet are on different sides of the balance line

It's time for some action!

Your cartoon characters have been standing around for too long! It's time they started moving. Now they can really create havoc! Drawing a moving figure is easy if you just keep on doing what you've been doing – starting with the basic shapes and only then getting stuck into the details.

Before you start to draw a moving character, ask a friend to be the model. Ask them to run, walk or creep and carefully study their movements. Where are their feet in relation to the head? Where are the arms and hands? What are the legs doing? Is the back rounded or straight?

Here are three easy first steps to add action to your cartoon.

How to make a character run

STEP 1 ▲
In pencil, draw the head then the body, legs and feet. Draw the arms and hands last.

STEP 2 ▲
Fill out the lines using shapes. Start with geometric shapes and then smooth and round them.

STEP 3 ▲
Add detail and movement lines. Go over with a felt-tipped pen and rub out the pencil lines.

Walking

Three easy steps...   *to a very brisk...*   *march. Note the arms*

Slouching

Keep head low...   *and back rounded...*   *for a great slouch!*

Jumping

If you can draw this...   *then turn it into this...*   *you can jump too!*

53

The secret of movement lines

Movement lines indicate – yes, you guessed it, movement. It is amazing how just a couple of tiny lines can help bring your cartoons to life. You can show movement and action by drawing small arcs, straight or slightly curved lines, clouds of dust, beads of sweat, shadows, splat patterns or a mixture of all six. Draw the lines using quick, light strokes, making sure that they do not touch the character. A movement line that comes in contact with the character gives the impression that the cartoon is static or being slowed down.

Cartoons with bounce

Small arcs near bottom and hands show they are moving around

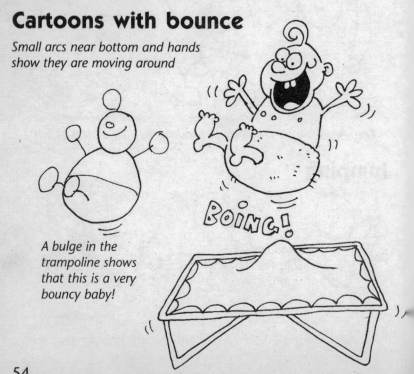

A bulge in the trampoline shows that this is a very bouncy baby!

BOING!

More ways to make things move

Beads of sweat

Small arcs around hands and feet

Zap lines and musical notes show the source of the music

Shadow beneath stereo shows it's bopping to the music as well

Curved parallel lines show the chopping action

This bird is so fast it raises dust

Pattern on the punchbag shows the power of this punch

Dots are fragments of bread flying out

Shadows show that the character is in mid-air

55

Making a flickerbook

Now's your chance to create your own animated cartoon by making a flickerbook. This is an effective way to bring your cartoons to life but it does require lots of drawing. Keep the pictures as simple as possible to start with!

STEP 1 ▶
You need a pad of plain, slightly transparent paper (this helps position your cartoons). Turn the pad upside down (bound side nearest you) and pencil-in a cartoon in the top right-hand corner of the last page.

STEP 2 ▶
On the second last page, draw the image again but slightly change it so that it will appear to have moved. Continue doing this, with small changes each time and still in pencil, on the next 25 pages. Always keep the action in the right-hand corner.

STEP 3 ▶

To check that your animation works, flick the pages of the pad from back to front with your thumb. Make any alterations and then go over your drawings with a fine felt-tipped pen.

STEP 4 ▶

Add details, or even shading and colour if you are feeling very ambitious, to your cartoons. Keep the details consistent in each frame. Plenty of movement lines will speed-up the action.

STEP 5 ▶

Settle back with a box of popcorn, flick the pages of the pad and enjoy the show.

Each page of your flicker cartoon is just like a frame in an animated cartoon. Here are some of the frames from Tim's flicker cartoon put side-by-side.

Drawing animals

Drawing animals is little different from the way cartoonists draw people. You start with the same basic shapes and then add the details. Because the shape of many animals is similar (for example, the basic patterns needed for a cat, dog and cow are identical), it is important that you get the details right. You have to know your animals. If you don't have an elephant or crocodile willing to model for you, then head for the library and find a reference book with lots of pictures. Here are some animal heads, each using a different basic shape, to get you in the mood.

Square dogs   *Triangular cats*   *Round monkeys*   *Oval frogs*

How to draw a panda

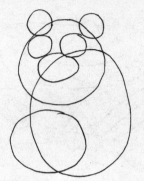

◀ **STEP 1**
Draw the shapes as shown in pencil. Make the body one and a half times larger than the head.

STEP 2 ▶
Add the arms and draw a rectangle for the mouth. Put small circles inside the ears.

◀ **STEP 3**
Draw in teeth, tail, eyes and a triangle for the nose. Add toes on the paws. Go over the lines shown with felt-tipped pen and, when dry, rub out unwanted pencil lines.

STEP 4 ▶
Draw pads on one hand and on the sole of the paw before filling in with solid black. Finishing touches are a few bristling hairs and some tufts of grass for the panda to sit on.

How to draw a frog

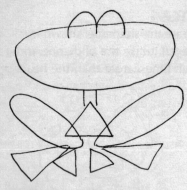

STEP 1 ▲

Draw the basic shapes in pencil. The head is as wide as the splayed legs, and is about half the frog's total height.

STEP 2 ▲

Draw ovals for the eyes and curved lines for its wide mouth and chin. Join the front feet to the body with four lines, and draw a line through the two large ovals.

STEP 3 ▲

Smooth and round the pencil lines as shown.

STEP 4 ▲

Draw webbed feet and add two dots for the eyes. Go over with a felt-tipped pen.

60

How to draw a cat

◀ **STEP 1**

Draw the basic shapes in pencil. Exaggerate the size of the pointy ear and make sure that the feet and paws closest are larger than those furthest away.

STEP 2 ▶

Draw the eye and below it draw a sideways 3 to create the mouth and jaw. Don't forget to give puss an elegant curvy tail.

◀ **STEP 3**

A small triangle is fine for the upturned nose. Draw a line to show the inside of the ear, then smooth and round all the lines.

STEP 4 ▶

Add whiskers and fur to the face, ear and chest, and draw toes on the paws. Go over the cartoon with a felt-tipped pen and, when dry, rub out pencil lines.

Animal faces

Look at this cartoon picture of a pig's face and then look at your own face in a mirror. Notice anything different, really different? You shouldn't, because in essence you and the pig have a lot in common (only face-wise of course). You both have two eyes, a mouth, a nose, cheeks, ears and eyebrows. When it comes to drawing most animal faces, you can rely on the skills you've used for drawing human faces. Yes, even when drawing an elephant!

Pig

STEP 1 ▲
Draw the circles and ovals for the face, eyes, cheeks, nose and ears.

STEP 2 ▲
Add detail to the ears, a broad smile and nostrils.

STEP 3 ▲
Draw curved lines for the eyebrows and chins. Go over with felt-tipped pen and rub out pencil lines.

Here are some more animal faces to practise. When you have mastered these, use the same techniques to create your own.

Dog

Elephant

Tiger

Trade secret

When you are drawing with a pencil or felt-tipped pen it's easy to smudge your cartoons with the side of your hand. To prevent this, rest the side of your drawing hand on a clean piece of paper placed over your drawing.

All animals are not the same

Animal faces may have a lot
in common but the rest of
their bodies is often wildly
different – in shape, size
and texture. Now you need
to look at these differences
and work them into your
cartoons. The last thing you
want is your cartoon dog to
be mistaken for a horse! The
sorts of things you should be
aware of are:

1 Head shape and size – we have done faces but what
about the head? Is it long, short, round, square, triangular,
wide or narrow? Look at how the head is joined to the
body. Does the animal have an
obvious neck or are the head and
body as one?

2 Eyes – their shape (round or
oval) and where they are
positioned are important. On
animals with long faces the eyes
are usually closer to the top of
the head. Also look to see if the
eyes are set close together or far
apart. Some animals such as cows
have long eyelashes that can be
exaggerated in your cartoons.

3 Ears – take note of their shape (floppy, pointed,
triangular or round), size and position. Are the ears on the
top of the head, to the sides or somewhere in between?

Close-ups

Whether you are drawing an animal in the distance or close-up, it is important to give an impression of the texture of their coat or skin. In cartoons, you don't have to cover a snake from end to end with scales or painstakingly draw every strand of hair in a lion's

mane (cartoons are for fun after all, not for scientific study). It is enough just to draw scales on a few small areas of the snake or to suggest long hair or fur with just a few quickly-drawn lines.

4 Nose – on some animals it is enough just to draw nostrils, but on others a full hooter is needed. The two basic nose shapes are triangular or round.

5 Mouth – before you look at the size and shape of a mouth, decide whether you need to draw it at all. On some animals the mouth is on the underside of a protruding jaw and barely visible. Often more important are the teeth – imagine drawing a crocodile and not showing its teeth!

Animals from different views

Drawing round-headed animals in profile or three-quarter view is the same as drawing human heads, as shown on pages 30-32. But long-nosed animals, like horses, are a little different.

◀ STEP 1

Draw the basic shapes to make the head. Note the position of the ears and eyes.

STEP 2 ▶

Add texture to the mane and nose. Draw in simple curved eyebrows. See how the eyebrow on the right falls beyond the outline of the head.

◀ STEP 3

Finish by drawing short, quick lines for the horse's coat and dots for the pupils. Fill in the nostrils.

Creatures great and small

In this chapter we take a further look into the animal kingdom. It is full of such weird and wonderful creatures that it could have been made for cartoonists.

How to draw a tarantula

◀ **STEP 1**

In pencil, draw the basic shapes. This arachnid is angry – look at his eyes!

STEP 2 ▶

Draw in the mouth, teeth and cheeks.

◀ **STEP 3**

Make the lines jagged to show its all-over covering of hair. Go over with a felt-tipped pen and rub out pencil lines.

STEP 4 ▶

Add stripes to the legs and black the inside of the mouth. To finish, make dots for the pupils.

Caterpillar

STEP 1 ▲

In pencil, draw overlapping circles for the segmented body, making them smaller closer to the tail. Draw the head.

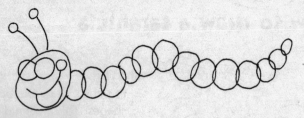

STEP 2 ▲

Add features to the face and a pair of antennae.

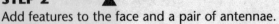
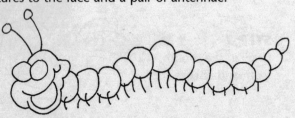

STEP 3 ▲

Draw masses of tiny legs down its body, but not on the final few segments.

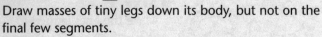

STEP 4 ▲

Draw the feet and details of the face. Lightly shade each segment as shown. Go over the pencil lines with felt-tipped pen.

Ladybird

◀ **STEP 1**
Draw an oval, divided as shown, for the basic shape. This shape can be used for any type of beetle.

STEP 2 ▶
Draw eyes, mouth and circles of varying size on the back.

◀ **STEP 3**
Add features to the face and draw the legs. No prizes for guessing this is a lady ladybird.

STEP 4 ▶
Go over the pencil lines with a felt-tipped pen and colour dots and face black. For a fun finishing touch, give her a set of high-heeled boots!

Backgrounds for your cartoon animals

Pasture

Jungle

Tree top

Seabed

Farm friends

Let's start with something so easy you could draw it with your eyes closed – well almost!

How to draw a sheep

STEP 1 ▶

Draw the basic shapes of the body and head in pencil. Note the size of the head and its position at the front of the body.

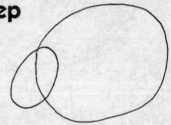

◀ ### STEP 2

Draw circles and ovals as shown (the head is turned toward you so the eyes are not in the middle). Add the short, spindly legs.

STEP 3 ▶

Draw the mouth then give the sheep an enormous woolly coat and two nostrils.

◀ ### STEP 4

Go over with a felt-tipped pen. Draw curvy lines on the body to make the sheep look rounded. Rub out pencil lines.

How to draw a pig

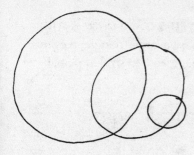

STEP 1 ▲

In pencil, draw three circles, as shown, for the snout, head and body. The head is quite large in relation to the body.

STEP 2 ▲

Draw rectangles for the legs, making sure that the legs farthest away are smallest. Create the face and ears using circles, ovals and curved lines.

STEP 3 ▲

Draw in the teeth, tongue, tight curly tail and trotters.

STEP 4 ▲

Go over the pencil lines with a felt-tipped pen adding nostrils, pupils, eyebrows and tufts of hair on the body. Colour the mouth as shown.

How to draw a chicken

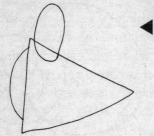

◄ STEP 1
Draw a large triangle, a dome shape and an oval in pencil.

STEP 2 ▶
Use a triangle and a circle to make the beak, and draw circles for the eyes. Inside the large triangle draw part of another triangle and part of an oval. Simple lines form the feet and claws.

◄ STEP 3
Still in pencil, round and curve the lines, as shown, and draw the comb. Finish the feet and claws.

STEP 4 ▶
Shape the ends of the wing and tail, and suggest feathers with curved lines. Go over your cartoon with a felt-tipped pen. The egg and a friendly cluck are the finishing touches.

And now for your masterpiece!

OK, that's the easy stuff over with! Let's get on now to the one animal everyone wishes they could draw well. Of course, it is the horse. Here's one Tim did earlier, in all its cartoonland glory. Do you think you are up to it? If you have coped so far you will be able to draw your own horse. Promise! Turn the page to find out how.

How to draw a horse

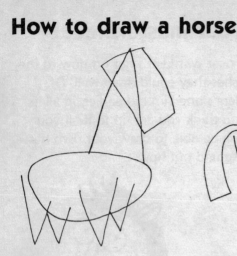

STEP 1 ▲

Draw the basic shape of the horse in pencil. The body is about as long as the neck.

STEP 2 ▲

Add the tail, ears, legs and hooves.

STEP 3 ▲

Pencil in a rough mane, and then carefully draw the face using the basic shape as a guide.

STEP 4 ▲

Round off the head and body and fill out the shape of the leg

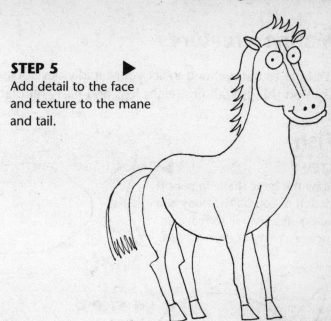

STEP 5 ▶
Add detail to the face
and texture to the mane
and tail.

STEP 6 ▶
You've almost finished. Go over your
cartoon in a felt-tipped pen, roughly
colour the mane and tail and fill in
the hooves. Add texture to the coat
with tiny lines and lightly shade
the inside of the legs.

*There! Your horse is
complete. Remember,
practice makes perfect!*

Marine creatures

It's time to get wet and inflict your rapidly developing skills on things with fins, eight legs and nasty reputations.

Fish

STEP 1 ▶

Draw the basic shape in pencil. Stretch or squash the body and exaggerate the tail to make an endless variety of different fish.

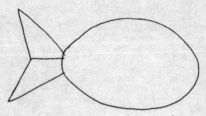

◀ **STEP 2**
Add fins, eye and wide mouth.

STEP 3 ▶

Round the fins and tail and adjust the shape of the head so that the upper jaw overhangs the lower jaw.

◀ **STEP 4**
Draw scales on the body and add texture to the fins and tail. Go over with a felt-tipped pen and rub out pencil lines.

Octopus

The problem here is finding space for all its tentacles. Don't sell your octopus short by giving him only six legs.

STEP 1 ▶

Draw the basic shapes for the head and body in pencil, then lightly sketch eight tentacles.

◀ STEP 2

Draw a smily face and add a fun detail. An octopus always looks good in a hat!

STEP 3 ▶

Round off the tentacles and add detail to the face.

◀ STEP 4

Fill the wide smile with teeth and go over your cartoon with a felt-tipped pen. Rub out pencil lines.

Penguin

Penguins are a firm favourite and they make great cartoon characters. See if you can draw a family of penguins.

STEP 1 ▶
Draw the two basic shapes shown here. Keep your pencil sharp!

◀ **STEP 2**
Add the flippers and fins and draw features on the face.

STEP 3 ▶
Draw a curved line across the penguin's tummy and a short, stumpy tail.

STEP 4 ▲
Add detail to the flippers and face. Colour in the body black, leaving a white space for the water line across the penguin's body.

80

Shark

This shark is angry, so don't hold back when it comes to drawing the steely stare and razor-sharp teeth.

STEP 1 ▶
Draw the basic shapes in pencil.

◀ **STEP 2**
Add fins, tail, eyes and angry eyebrows, and then what looks like a big, cheesy grin.

STEP 3 ▶
Bang, there goes the smile – in come the teeth. Shape the fins.

◀ **STEP 4**
Shape the mouth to make it look as though the shark has drawn back its lips, and draw lines for the gills. Go over your cartoon with a felt-tipped pen and then find somewhere safe to hide!

Deep in the jungle

From farm to sea to jungle, cartoonists really get around!
There are some wonderful jungle animals to draw. An
elephant's trunk, lion's mane or monkey's tail make them
easy subjects for the cartoonist's pen. Sometimes their
features are so peculiar there is no need to exaggerate!

Elephant

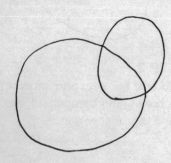

STEP 1 ▲

Draw, in pencil, the basic
shapes. The body is about
twice the size of the head.

STEP 2 ▲

More basic shapes create the
trunk, eyes, chubby cheek, ears
and stumpy legs.

STEP 3 ▲

Add shape to the ears and
draw the tusks.

STEP 4 ▲

Add a tail, toenails, nostrils, eyes
and eyebrows then go over the
lines with a felt-tipped pen.

How to make a tracing

Use this technique if you want to copy a picture, design or lettering on to a piece of drawing paper.

STEP 1 ▶

Place tracing paper (cooking parchment paper or thin layout paper also works) over the original image. Draw over the image with a thick pencil.

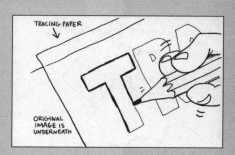

STEP 2 ▶

Lift off the tracing paper and turn it over so that the outline is face down. Heavily shade over the back of the outline with a pencil.

STEP 3 ▶

Turn the tracing paper over (the outline is now face up) and place it, in position, on to your drawing paper. Firmly draw over the outline with pencil.

STEP 4 ▶

Lift off the tracing paper to see a copy of the original image, right way round!

Monkey business starts here

◀ **STEP 1**

Draw the basic shapes in pencil. Cartoon monkeys are made up of ovals, a circle and an oblong.

STEP 2 ▶

Join the hands and feet to the body and draw a long tail. Divide the head as shown, and draw ears and eyes.

◀ **STEP 3**

Add more features to the face and flesh out the arms, legs and tail with parallel lines.

◀ **STEP 4**

Draw three fingers on each hand and three toes on each foot. Round the body to form its bottom.

STEP 5 ▶

Add detail to the face and ears. Give him a cheeky look!

◀ **STEP 6**

Give the monkey some fur – just a few clumps of tiny lines will do it. Shading around the feet shows that monkey's on the ground, not swinging around.

A crocodile, and make it snappy

▼ STEP 1

Draw the basic shapes in pencil, making the body just a little longer than the head. The tail is a back-to-front S-shape.

▼ STEP 2

Add features to the face and draw two circles for the croc's feet. Note how the front foot is almost in line with the narrow, oval eyes.

▼ STEP 3

Draw scales along the top of its body and a little way down its tail, and ridges across its nose. Add shape to the feet.

▼ STEP 4

Draw three claws on each foot, nostrils and dots in the corner of the eyes (for extra slyness). Then comes the best bit – a zigzag line for the teeth.

▼ STEP 5

Go over with a felt-tipped pen and rub out pencil lines. Draw scales on the body and suggest the flicking tail with movement lines. Who'd have believed it – a smiling crocodile!

Smiling croc too hard to believe? Tim thought so, too. He quickly penned this one for you to try. Watch out, those teeth are SHARP!

87

This lion is a roaring success

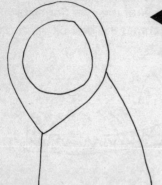

◀ **STEP 1**

Draw the basic shapes in pencil. The head and mane should be about the same size as the body.

STEP 2 ▶

Draw eyes (very angry eyes!), nose, ears, rear leg and paws.

◀ **STEP 3**

Add more detail to the face and ears, and draw a shaggy mane. Draw in lines for one of the front legs.

STEP 4 ▶

Line the mouth with sharp teeth and give the lion a beard, toes and tail.

STEP 5 ▶

Colour in the nose
and the back of the
mouth, give him
some hair and a
pom-pom on his
tail. Small dots
around his nose are
the whiskers. Finish
him off with a
mighty roar!

Trade secret

*Things get smaller the farther away they get and larger
when closer. Using this fact in your cartoons can transform their
impact. In the cartoon on the left, King Kong's foot is bigger than
his head – strange but very effective! To achieve this, first draw a
triangle and put all the character's basic shapes inside it. It works!*

Parrot fashion

STEP 1
Draw the basic shapes in pencil. Note how high the head is on the body.

STEP 2
Draw the eyes in line with the far wing, and a line from the parrot's right eye to the bottom of its head. Don't forget its tail!

STEP 3
Shape the wings and tail and pile the plumage on his head. Draw the beak. When you're happy with your cartoon, draw the movement lines.

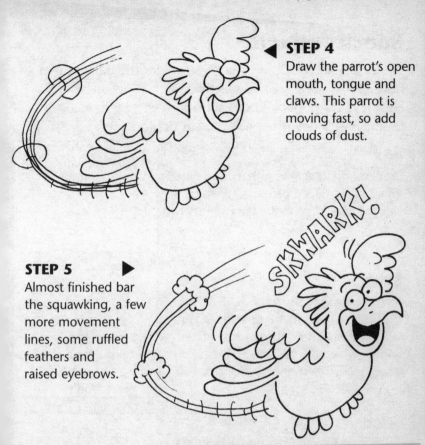

STEP 4
Draw the parrot's open mouth, tongue and claws. This parrot is moving fast, so add clouds of dust.

STEP 5
Almost finished bar the squawking, a few more movement lines, some ruffled feathers and raised eyebrows.

Beak peak

Once you've got the basic bird shape off pat, it's very easy to draw almost any type of bird. All you have to do is change the beak, lengthen or shorten the wings, sharpen the claws and adjust the fancy plumage. Here's a selection of beaks and bills that may come in handy.

Hawk

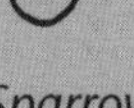
Sparrow

Duck

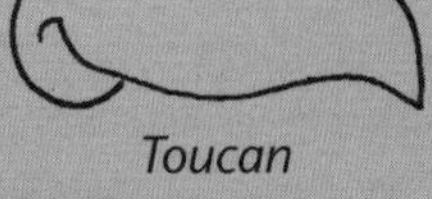
Toucan

Special effects

You've drawn your characters, you've got the background – now all you need is some weather! Rain, wind, snow and lightning are popular in cartoonland. But how to achieve them? Here's how the professionals do it...

Rain

Draw short, quick lines with a fine-pointed pencil or felt-tipped pen. It is important that the lines all go in the same direction.

Snow

If you're going to show snow, then you may as well make them giant snowflakes. Vary the size of the circles to add interest and show depth – the largest flakes seem closer, the smallest ones farther away.

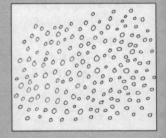

Wind

Swirling, sweeping lines are the best way of showing a howling wind. But don't forget that the wind will affect characters and objects in your cartoon – hair will be blown about, leaves will be swept away and trees will bend.

Lightning

Use this not only to represent a violent thunderstorm but also to signify that one of your characters is angry. Simply draw a single cloud with lightning strokes right above the character's head.

6 Nice and nasty

Until now all the cartoons you have been drawing have been based on "real" things – people, objects, animals and background scenes. Now it's time to unbolt the door to your imagination so you can make your dreams come true and create your own fantastic creatures. Nice ones as well as nasty ones!

Where to start? For the nasties, you could combine animals you have already learnt to draw for some horrible hybrids. Perhaps they come from another planet! Or use your favourite aliens, monsters or extinct animals from films or books. Draw in plenty of details like scaly skin and sharp fangs. Let your imagination run riot! Don't forget you can also conjure up nice things!

Turn the page for Tim's ideas of some nice and nasty cartoons...

An alien has landed!

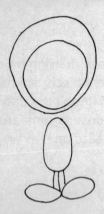

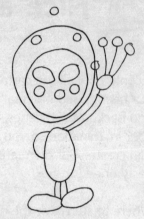

STEP 1 ▲

Draw the basic shapes in pencil. Squash or stretch them to create your own alien being.

STEP 2 ▲

More simple shapes form the arms, hands and face.

BEEP!
BEEP!
I COME
IN PEACE!
BEEP!

STEP 3 ▲

Draw the mouth, nose, neck and finish the hand. Give the alien a pair of space boots.

STEP 4 ▲

Add pupils, chin and detail to the boots. Go over with a felt-tipped pen. Your alien has landed!

Watch out, a vampire's about

STEP 1 ▲
Draw two ovals and a triangle in pencil.

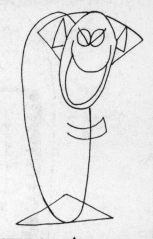

STEP 2 ▲
More shapes form the collar, ears, eyes, mouth and arm.

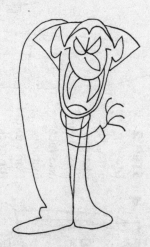

STEP 3 ▲
Give the vampire a slick-back hair style, add detail to the face and draw a hand. Round the edges on the coat.

STEP 4 ▲
Go over with a felt-tipped pen and rub out pencil lines.

Dr Frankenstein's monster

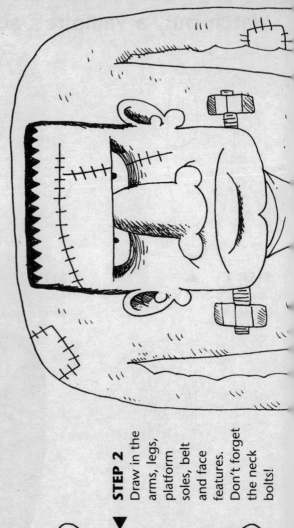

STEP 1
Draw the basic shapes for the bulky body in pencil.

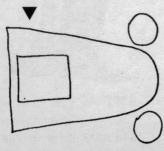

STEP 2
Draw in the arms, legs, platform soles, belt and face features. Don't forget the neck bolts!

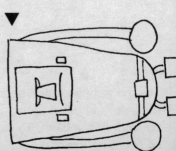

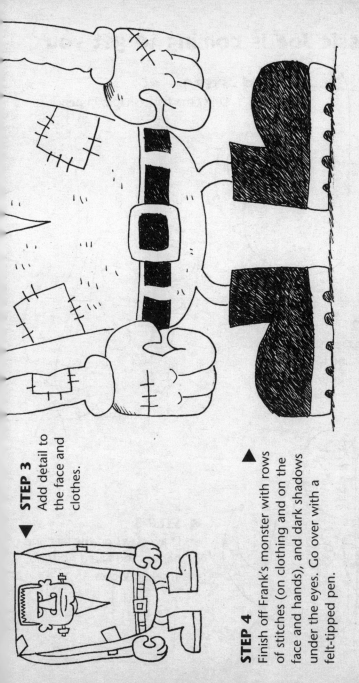

STEP 3

Add detail to the face and clothes.

STEP 4

Finish off Frank's monster with rows of stitches (on clothing and on the face and hands), and dark shadows under the eyes. Go over with a felt-tipped pen.

Jurassic Joe is coming to get you

◀ **STEP 1**
Draw the basic shapes in pencil.

STEP 2 ▶
Add legs, arms and hands.
A curvy line forms the
snout and mouth.

◀ **STEP 3**
Draw claws on the feet and
hands. Add flared nostrils
and angry eyes.

STEP 4 ▲
Fill the mouth with sharp teeth.

STEP 5 ▲
Give Joe a double-chin, a bumpy snout, eyeballs, nostrils and triangular spines along his back.

STEP 6 ▶
Go over with a felt-tipped pen and colour the inside of the mouth. Put in some scales and draw movement lines and a shadow below his body. Rub out pencil lines.

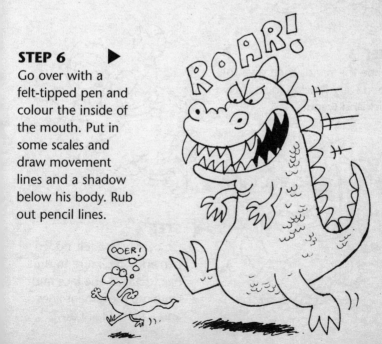

Time to call the Good Fairy

That's enough of the cartoon nasties – it's time for some much friendlier made-up cartoon characters.

STEP 1 ▶
Draw the basic shapes in pencil.

◀ **STEP 2**
More basic shapes form the shoulders, wings, arms and legs. Draw features on the face.

STEP 3 ▶
Shape the hands then give the Good Fairy flowing locks, frilly frock and wand.

◀ **STEP 4**
Go over with a felt-tipped pen adding texture to the hair, detail to the face and clothing, movement lines and a trail of fairy dust.

Princess Perfect

STEP 1 ▶

Draw the basic shapes in pencil.

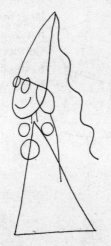

◀ STEP 2

Circles, ovals and lines form the face, hair, shoulders and hands.

STEP 3 ▶

Round and shape the gown and trailing scarf. Draw arms. Add detail to the face (long eyelashes and pert nose are a must) hair and hands.

◀ STEP 4

Rub out unwanted lines and finish the hair. Go over with felt-tipped pen and do the finishing touches.

Catwalk Queen

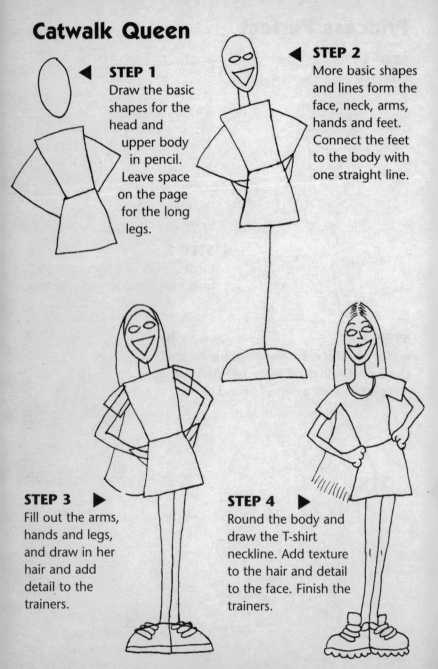

◀ **STEP 1**
Draw the basic shapes for the head and upper body in pencil. Leave space on the page for the long legs.

◀ **STEP 2**
More basic shapes and lines form the face, neck, arms, hands and feet. Connect the feet to the body with one straight line.

STEP 3 ▶
Fill out the arms, hands and legs, and draw in her hair and add detail to the trainers.

STEP 4 ▶
Round the body and draw the T-shirt neckline. Add texture to the hair and detail to the face. Finish the trainers.

102

A family of models

You can adapt the basic shapes as shown in steps 1 and 2 of Catwalk Queen to create a whole gallery of fashion models. It takes only simple changes to dress your models in jeans, shorts or long dresses. Look at page 26 for hairstyle ideas and page 47 for different shoe styles.

◀ **STEP 5**
Go over with a felt-tipped pen and add more texture to the hair. A nice touch is to decorate the clothes.

Nice and nasty

Spooky backgrounds for your cartoon characters

Haunted castle

Laboratory

104

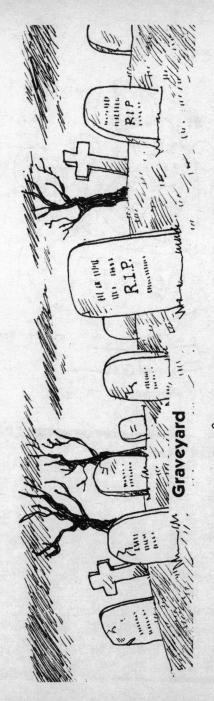

Graveyard

Monster under
the bed!

Borrowed bodies

Imagination left you? There's always another way of inventing creatures. Like Dr Frankenstein, assemble bits from different characters or animals. There's no end to the number of mix-ups! And all of them are horrible. Don't forget to give your creation a name.

PIG'S SNOUT

SHARK'S FIN

MONKEY TAIL

LION'S TEETH

CROCODILE CLAWS

ELEPHANT FEET

Dr Tim Frankenstein's "Pigleocro-cothump".

Flip-flap-flop cartoon book

Make a book using three sheets of paper folded in half and stapled down the folded edge. Divide the front and back of each page into three using a ruler and pencil. Draw a cartoon face on each page making sure the hair and eyes are in the top third; the nose and ears in the middle third; and the mouth, chin and neck in the bottom third. Cut along the lines almost to the fold. You'll laugh when you turn the pages!

Comic strips

Cartoons are great on their own but they take on a whole different meaning when you put a lot of them together. They make – you guessed – a comic strip. Tim has done one for us here. It tells the story of a singing alien that takes all his clothes off. Weird or what! But that's the good thing about comic strips – you can use your cartoon characters to tell any story you like, the weirder the better!

Creating a cartoon strip is not as difficult as you may think. The important things are: work out your story first, use very few characters, and draw it bit by bit. We have more on all of this coming up. Sharpen your pencil and good luck!

The six golden rules

1 Try to think in pictures. In cartoons, the pictures are the most important thing. You shouldn't have to rely on words to tell the story.

2 It can help to rough out each box of your cartoon on a separate piece of paper. This makes it easy to shuffle the pages and to remove or introduce new ideas.

3 To start, create characters that are easy to draw. You may have to draw them lots of times in different positions.

4 Allow room for speech bubbles and sound effects (see page 114). Your cartoon will most probably be read from left to right, so speech bubbles must in the right order.

5 Only show what you need to show. Draw characters in close-up and focus in on the important things.

6 Don't let the background dominate your characters.

Speech bubbles

FIRST WRITE WHAT YOU WANT YOUR CHARACTER TO SAY IN CLEAR CAPITALS.

THEN DRAW A BUBBLE AROUND THE WRITING.

DO A POINT TOWARDS THE SPEAKING CHARACTER.

OR THEY COULD JUST BE THINKING ABOUT SOMETHING.

These are handy devices where you write the words that your characters speak or think. Oval bubbles are for normal talking, cloud-like ones are for thoughts while jagged, star-burst bubbles are for sound effects or to show that someone is shouting.

Where do you get ideas from?

From just about everywhere is the short answer. Something funny may happen on the school bus, while you're at a skate park, chewing on a fish finger or soaking in the bath.

This is the wonderful thing about being a cartoonist – you can get ideas from absolutely everywhere! A cartoonist is constantly on the lookout for weird, odd-ball and hysterical situations. But if you think that your corner of the world is short on inspiration, then there's always the television, films, books and your own vivid imagination.

The problem with ideas is that if you don't write them down they vanish into thin air. So no matter where you are or what you're doing, if you see a great cartoon idea, write it down or draw a quick sketch.

How to make a three-frame cartoon

Follow these steps to create your first cartoon strip! Okay, so it's only a three-box cartoon but once you've mastered this then longer, grander, madder and more involved cartoons will be a doddle. Draw everything in pencil first.

◀ STEP 1

Write down your idea for a cartoon, its characters and its setting. Your story should have a beginning, middle and end. The ending should have a funny punch line. Break the story into three and make sure each part has some of the action.

◀ STEP 2

Draw the three frames and make them at least twice as large as you want them (you can always reduce it when photocopying). Work out where you need speech bubbles.

◀ STEP 3

Using just basic shapes, rough out your cartoon and draw speech/thought bubbles and star bursts for sound effects. This stage is important so keep fiddling with your cartoon until it is just right.

STEP 4
Pencil in the speech and lettering and check the spelling. Adjust the sizes of the speech bubbles if necessary.

STEP 5
Add detail to the cartoon, giving your characters lots of expression. Put in any background scene. Use cross-hatching to create texture and areas of shadow. Draw in movement lines.

STEP 6
Go over your cartoon with felt-tipped pen and rub out pencil lines. Congratulate yourself – you've done your first cartoon strip!

PS Don't forget to sign your name – you're a cartoonist now!

Lettering

Crazy lettering can bring your cartoons and your characters to life. But like backgrounds and details, you should add lettering sparingly so that it doesn't dominate your comic strip.

How to get the most from lettering

1 What do you want to use it for? To title a cartoon, to name a character or to show an action or sound effect?

2 Whatever you want to write, keep it short and write it out in capital letters (cartoonists usually use capital letters because they're easier to read) on a separate piece of paper.

3 Check how much room you have for the lettering. Do this by placing a piece of tracing paper over your cartoon and then roughing-out the lettering on the tracing paper.

4 Design (and this is the best bit) a lettering style that matches the character or the cartoon. Remember, cartoon lettering looks much more lively when it's a bit of a mess. Do the lettering in pencil and, only when you're completely happy with it, go over it with a felt-tipped pen.

This lettering is really easy to do and it's perfect for old Wobbly Will here or for an underwater cartoon

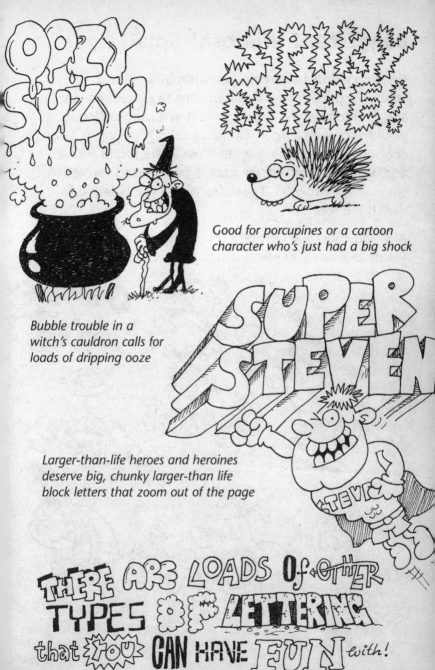

Good for porcupines or a cartoon character who's just had a big shock

Bubble trouble in a witch's cauldron calls for loads of dripping ooze

Larger-than-life heroes and heroines deserve big, chunky larger-than life block letters that zoom out of the page

113

Bang! Zap! Whoosh! Splat!

Creating words to describe sounds is a fun part of cartooning. From now on listen hard to everything you hear and decide how you would write it in a cartoon. How would you write a door slamming, a baby talking, a sausage cooking? The first thing to do is make the sound yourself and work out which letter sounds you need to "write" that word. It's even better if you also design the lettering to match the sound.

And you know the best bit? You can spell these sound effect words any way you want!

Use symbols instead of letters when words or sound effects might not be very polite!

Caricature

A caricature is when you highlight certain features – for example, the shape of a face or the size of a nose – when drawing a picture of a real person. Exaggerating features is used all the time in cartooning, but the difference here is that you're drawing someone who really exists.

The easiest way to draw a caricature is to start from a photograph. Friends just won't sit still long enough for you to have a really good look at their worst features. These are things you have to look out for:

1 Shape of the head.
2 Type of hair.
3 Size and shape of mouth, teeth, nose, ears, jaw, forehead, eyes, chin.
4 Other distinguishing features like freckles, scars, glasses.

Find which of these is the most obvious feature and then exaggerate it. Don't go overboard and try to highlight lots of features. Concentrate on just a couple.

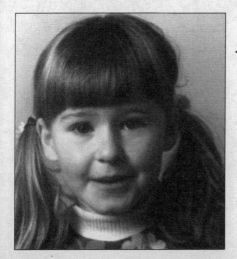

◀ **STEP 1**
Find a good, clear photograph of your subject and spend some time studying it. The most obvious features here are the small button nose, straight fringe and dimpled chin.

Caricature

◀ STEP 2

In pencil, draw the outline of the head and then draw the nose, chin and fringe. Do these first so they dominate, then go on to draw the rest of the face, neck, shoulders and hair.

STEP 3 ▶

Do the details as you would for a normal cartoon, but underplay those that distract from the main features. Go over your caricature with a felt-tipped pen.

Funny not hurtful

Caricatures are meant to be funny, not hurtful so try to be sensitive to your model's feelings. If they have a real thing about the braces on their teeth, ignore them and play up something else instead.

Drawing kit extras

If you want to experiment with different media, here are some other bits and pieces you might want.

Wax crayons

Though it is impossible to draw detail with these chunky things, they are great for filling in backgrounds, adding bursts of colour and for practising loose, flowing lines. But be warned – they are impossible to rub out.

Charcoal

Now we're talking serious cartooning. Charcoal sticks can be used for drawing strong, dark lines and sweeping backgrounds. Smudge the lines to soften them and create spooky effects. Charcoal sticks break easily but they are cheap and even the broken bits have a use.

Fountain pen

You've most probably got one of these for your school-work but if you can use it as well for cartooning, do so – fountain pens are great for drawing cartoons. By varying the pressure on the nib, you can create lots of different and lively lines. No need to warn you about smudging – you know all about that.

So you want to be a cartoonist?

And who can blame you for wanting to spend your time looking for the funny side of things, dreaming up jokes and creating odd characters? What's the secret to becoming a fulltime cartoonist?

According to Tim, the key to success is practice. You've just got to keep on drawing anything and everything until you can almost put together a cartoon with your eyes shut.

Here's our Tim hard at work as usual. You don't have to stick your tongue out if you don't want to

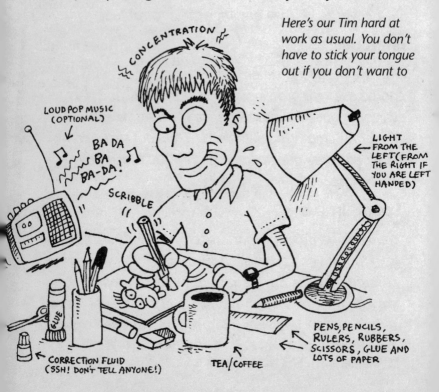

CONCENTRATION

LOUD POP MUSIC (OPTIONAL)

BA DA BA BA-DA!

SCRIBBLE

LIGHT FROM THE LEFT (FROM THE RIGHT IF YOU ARE LEFT HANDED)

GLUE

CORRECTION FLUID (SSH! DON'T TELL ANYONE!)

TEA/COFFEE

PENS, PENCILS, RULERS, RUBBERS, SCISSORS, GLUE AND LOTS OF PAPER

Once you understand how to make cartoons (and we hope you have, this far into the book) it's then a matter of developing your own unique style and a family of favourite characters.

Crucial in this is your sketchbook. A cartoonist without a sketchbook full of finished cartoons or ideas-in-progress is just not natural. Your sketchbook is what you will use to show people just how great a cartoonist you are. As your cartoons improve, select the best ones and carefully keep them in a portfolio – that's a smart collection of your best work that you can use to show to people.

And talking about work – where do cartoonists work? They can work for newspapers, magazines, book publishers, stationery and greeting-card companies, and in advertising, television and film. Sometimes jobs are advertised but the usual way is to send copies of your best cartoons to possible employers. With luck they'll ask you to come in and show off your sparkling personality and sharp sense of humour.

Though many cartoonists go to art school or university to study illustration or one of the other graphic arts, it is not essential. Many famous cartoonists have never been trained, they just followed their instincts. Because the cartoon world is one where rules are meant to be broken and where off-the-planet ideas are welcomed, there's lots of opportunity for you to express your own personality – whoever you are, wherever you live.

Whether you stick to drawing cartoons for your own pleasure, or opt for a career in cartooning, just remember that it's always meant to be **FUN!**

Want to know more?

Useful addresses • Websites

The following organisations can help you.

UNITED KINGDOM

The Cartoon Art Trust (CAT)
Almost alone in the United
Kingdom, this group runs
classes, courses and lectures
in cartooning – and many
of them are specifically for
children. In partnership, they
organise cartoon fairs. CAT's
goal is to open a museum of
cartooning art.

CAT
New House
67-68 Hatton Garden
London EC1N 8JY
Tel: 0171 405 4717

Information on upcoming
events and happenings in the
cartoon world can be found at –
http://www.atreides.demon.co.uk
or try –
http://www.cartoonet.net

AUSTRALIA

*Australian Black & White
Artist's Club Inc.*
PO Box 318
Strawberry Hills
NSW 2012
Tel: 02 96017646

Australian Cartoon School
1st floor
421 King Georges Road
Beverley Hills
NSW 2209
Tel: 02 9547 2861

WEB WANDERING

Though there are few
instructional cartooning sites
on the web, you will find
samples of the work of
cartoonists from around the
world. Many cartoonists use
the web as a way of
advertising and show-casing
their work. Simply search
under the word **cartoonists**.

Index

Index

ACTIVATORS

All you need to know

0 340 715162	Astronomy	£3.99	☐
0 340 715197	Ballet	£3.99	☐
0 340 715847	Birdwatching	£3.99	☐
0 340 715189	Cartooning	£3.99	☐
0 340 715200	Computers Unlimited	£3.99	☐
0 340 715111	Cycling	£3.99	☐
0 340 715219	Drawing	£3.99	☐
0 340 715138	Football	£3.99	☐
0 340 715146	The Internet	£3.99	☐
0 340 715170	Riding	£3.99	☐
0 340 715235	Skateboarding	£3.99	☐
0 340 71512X	Swimming	£3.99	☐

Turn the page to find out how to order these books.

more info • more tips • more fun!

ORDER FORM

Books in the Activators series are available at your local bookshops, or can be ordered direct from the publisher. A complete list of titles is given on the previous page. Just tick the titles you want and complete the details below. Prices and availability are subject to change without prior notice.

Please enclose a cheque or postal order made payable to Bookpoint Ltd, and send to: Hodder Children's Books, Cash Sales Dept, Bookpoint, 39 Milton Park, Abingdon, Oxon OX14 4TD. Email address: orders@bookpoint.co.uk.

If you would prefer to pay by credit card, our call centre team would be delighted to take your order buy telephone. Our direct line is 01235 400414 (lines open 9.00 am – 6.00 pm, Monday to Saturday; 24-hour message answering service). Alternatively you can send a fax on 01235 400454.

Title .... First name .... Surname ....

Address ....

....

....

Daytime tel .... Postcode.....................................

If you would prefer to post a credit card order, please complete the following.

Please debit my Visa/Access/Diner's Card/American Express (delete as applicable) card number:

Signature ....

Expiry Date ....

If you would NOT like to receive further information on our products, please tick ☐ .